SACREDSPACE

6 MARCH 2022 TO 16 APRIL 2022

FROM THE WEBSITE WWW.SACREDSPACE.IE
PRAYER FROM THE IRISH JESUITS

ISBN: 9781788124942

Scripture quotations are from New Revised Standard Version Bible,
National Council of the Churches of Christ in the United States of America.
Used by permission. All rights reserved worldwide.
www.nrsvbibles.org

Weekly reflections are taken from books published by Messenger Publications.
For more information go to www.messenger.ie

Designed by Messenger Publications Design Department
Typeset in Adobe Caslon Pro & Avant Garde
Cover Image: Liam O'Connell SJ
Printed by GPS Colour Graphics

Messenger Publications,
37 Leeson Place, Dublin D02 E5V0, Ireland
www.messenger.ie

CONTENTS

Sacred Space Prayer

Bless all who worship you, almighty God,
from the rising of the sun to its setting:
from your goodness enrich us,
by your love inspire us,
by your Spirit guide us,
by your power protect us,
in your mercy receive us,
now and always.

How to Use This Book

During each week of Lent, begin by reading the 'Something to think and pray about each day this week'. Then go through the 'Presence of God', 'Freedom' and 'Consciousness' steps to help you prepare yourself to hear the Word of God speaking to you. In the next step, 'The Word', turn to the Scripture reading for each day of the week. Inspiration points are provided if you need them. Then return to the 'Conversation' and 'Conclusion' steps. Follow this process every day of Lent.

The Lent retreat at the back of this book follows a similar structure: an invitation to experience stillness, a Scripture passage and reflection points, and suggestions for prayer; you might find it useful to move back and forth between the daily reflections and the retreat.

6–12 March 2022

Something to think and pray about each day this week:

For the Christian, the season of Lent and Easter tells of a God who intervened in human history in an unimaginable way. He didn't come to a perfect time or a perfect place. In some sense, I'd love if he intervened in our times to show us how to deal with the challenges of the Internet and social media! The one thing for sure though, is that he entered the chaos of people's lives and the chaos of our world.

Let us not be afraid of the chaos that is often around us and within us. In particular, let us not be afraid of the chaos we see in the lives of others: the homeless person, the refugee, the person who is recovering in hospital. If God entered our chaos let us not be afraid to step into the chaos of those we serve and love.

Alan Hilliard, *Dipping into Lent*

The Presence of God

Lord, help me to be fully alive to your holy presence. Enfold me in your love. Let my heart become one with yours.

My soul longs for your presence, Lord. When I turn my thoughts to you, I find peace and contentment.

Freedom

Your death on the cross has set me free. I can live joyously and freely without fear of death. Your mercy knows no bounds.

Consciousness

At this moment, Lord, I turn my thoughts to you.
I will leave aside my chores and preoccupations.
I will take rest and refreshment in your presence.

The Word

The word of God comes down to us through the Scriptures.

May the Holy Spirit enlighten my mind and my heart to respond to the Gospel teachings:

to love my neighbour as myself,

to care for my sisters and brothers in Christ.

(Please turn to the Scripture on the following pages. Inspiration points are there, should you need them. When you are ready, return here to continue.)

Conversation

Begin to talk to Jesus about the Scripture you have just read. What part of it strikes a chord in you? Perhaps the words of a friend – or some story you have heard recently – will slowly rise to the surface of your consciousness. If so, does the story throw light on what the Scripture passage may be saying to you?

Conclusion

I thank God for these moments we have spent together and for any insights I have been given concerning the text.

Sunday 6 March
First Sunday of Lent
Luke 4:1–13

Jesus, full of the Holy Spirit, returned from the Jordan and was led by the Spirit in the wilderness, where for forty days he was tempted by the devil. He ate nothing at all during those days, and when they were over, he was famished. The devil said to him, 'If you are the Son of God, command this stone to become a loaf of bread.' Jesus answered him, 'It is written, "One does not live by bread alone."'

Then the devil led him up and showed him in an instant all the kingdoms of the world. And the devil said to him, 'To you I will give their glory and all this authority; for it has been given over to me, and I give it to anyone I please. If you, then, will worship me, it will all be yours.' Jesus answered him, 'It is written,

"Worship the Lord your God,
 and serve only him."'

Then the devil took him to Jerusalem, and placed him on the pinnacle of the temple, saying to him, 'If you are the Son of God, throw yourself down from here, for it is written,

"He will command his angels concerning you,
 to protect you",

and

"On their hands they will bear you up,

so that you will not dash your foot against a stone."'

Jesus answered him, 'It is said, "Do not put the Lord your God to the test."' When the devil had finished every test, he departed from him until an opportune time.

- That Jesus was tested throughout his ministry was widely held in early Christianity. The Letter to the Hebrews tells us, 'For we do not have a high priest (Jesus) who is unable to sympathise with our weakness, but we have one who in every respect has been tested as we are, yet without sin.'

Monday 7 March
Matthew 25:31–46

'When the Son of Man comes in his glory, and all the angels with him, then he will sit on the throne of his glory. All the nations will be gathered before him, and he will separate people one from another as a shepherd separates the sheep from the goats, and he will put the sheep at his right hand and the goats at the left. Then the king will say to those at his right hand, "Come, you that are blessed by my Father, inherit the kingdom prepared for you from the foundation of the world; for I was hungry and you gave me food, I was thirsty and you gave me something to drink, I was a stranger and you welcomed me, I was naked and you gave me clothing, I was sick and you took care of me, I was in prison and you visited me." Then the righteous will answer him, "Lord, when was it that we saw you hungry and gave you food, or thirsty and gave you something to drink? And when was it that we saw you a stranger and welcomed you, or naked and gave you clothing? And when was it that we saw you sick or in prison and visited you?" And the king will answer them, "Truly I tell you, just as you did it to one of the least of these who are members of my family, you did it to me." Then he will say to those at his left hand, "You that are accursed, depart from me into the eternal fire prepared for the devil and his angels; for I was hungry and you gave me no food, I was thirsty and you gave me nothing to drink, I was a stranger and you did not welcome me, naked and you did not give me clothing, sick and in prison and you did not visit me." Then they also will answer, "Lord, when was it that we saw you hungry or thirsty or a stranger or naked or sick or in prison, and did not take care of you?" Then he will answer them, "Truly I tell you, just as you did not do it to one of the least of these, you did not do it to me." And these will go away into eternal punishment, but the righteous into eternal life.'

- This parable of the sheep and the goats is not about the future, but about opening my eyes here and now to the needs of my neighbour – the hungry, the homeless, the refugee, the isolated lonely ones.

Jesus identifies with each one. If I turn away from my brothers and sisters in need, I am turning away from my brother Jesus.

Tuesday 8 March
Matthew 6:7–15

'When you are praying, do not heap up empty phrases as the Gentiles do; for they think that they will be heard because of their many words. Do not be like them, for your Father knows what you need before you ask him.

'Pray then in this way:
Our Father in heaven,
hallowed be your name.
Your kingdom come.
Your will be done,
on earth as it is in heaven.
Give us this day our daily bread.
And forgive us our debts,
as we also have forgiven our debtors.
And do not bring us to the time of trial,
but rescue us from the evil one.
For if you forgive others their trespasses, your
heavenly Father will also forgive you; but if you do
not forgive others, neither will your Father forgive
your trespasses.'

• Are you having difficulty praying just now? Maybe you are confused, annoyed, daydreaming. Try to be still for a few moments. Do you not know what to say? Try the prayer that Jesus offers here, the Our Father, praying it slowly, or just be still and silent in the Lord's presence. Prayer is a time of relaxing into the mystery of God's love, letting go of tensions and worries for this period of time.

Wednesday 9 March
Luke 11:29–32
When the crowds were increasing, he began to say, 'This generation is an evil generation; it asks for a sign, but no sign will be given to it except the sign of Jonah. For just as Jonah became a sign to the people of Nineveh, so the Son of Man will be to this generation. The queen of the South will rise at the judgement with the people of this generation and condemn them, because she came from the ends of the earth to listen to the wisdom of Solomon, and see, something greater than Solomon is here! The people of Nineveh will rise up at the judgement with this generation and condemn it, because they repented at the proclamation of Jonah, and see, something greater than Jonah is here!'

- Jonah is the sign of God's care for all. His call was to go to a far country who did not know him or his God. He is also a sign of God's care for us individually – his care was for Jonah's safety. Jonah's strength was in his trust in God. Prayer is a time of allowing trust in God to grow and become a central part of our being.

Thursday 10 March
Matthew 7:7–12

'Ask, and it will be given to you; search, and you will find; knock, and the door will be opened for you. For everyone who asks receives, and everyone who searches finds, and for everyone who knocks, the door will be opened. Is there anyone among you who, if your child asks for bread, will give a stone? Or if the child asks for a fish, will give a snake? If you then, who are evil, know how to give good gifts to your children, how much more will your Father in heaven give good things to those who ask him!

'In everything do to others as you would have them do to you; for this is the law and the prophets.'

* Prayer time is never wasted. Good things come in prayer even if they are maybe not what we asked for. Prayer opens the heart to good things from God. Be grateful at the end of prayer for time spent with the God. Prayer time is always productive by making us people of more love. True prayer brings peace of mind and heart. It also brings the peace of knowing we are loved and of being called into following the Lord.

Friday 11 March
Matthew 5:20–26

For I tell you, unless your righteousness exceeds that of the scribes and Pharisees, you will never enter the kingdom of heaven.

'You have heard that it was said to those of ancient times, "You shall not murder"; and "whoever murders shall be liable to judgement." But I say to you that if you are angry with a brother or sister, you will be liable to judgement; and if you insult a brother or sister, you will be liable to the council; and if you say, "You fool", you will be liable to the hell of fire. So when you are offering your gift at the altar, if you remember that your brother or sister has something against you, leave your gift there before the altar and go; first be reconciled to your brother or sister, and then come and offer your gift. Come to terms quickly with your accuser while you are on the way to court with him, or your accuser may hand you over to the judge, and the judge to the guard, and you will be thrown into prison. Truly I tell you, you will never get out until you have paid the last penny.'

- True religion is the religion of the heart. Jesus saw the good in the Pharisees but challenged them against any hypocrisy. He goes on to encourage us to live by one of the most difficult situations in life – to forgive and be reconciled with others.

- Pay attention to the way we deal with each other; seek reconciliation with each other above all.

Saturday 12 March
Matthew 5:43–48

'You have heard that it was said, "You shall love your neighbour and hate your enemy." But I say to you, Love your enemies and pray for those who persecute you, so that you may be children of your Father in heaven; for he makes his sun rise on the evil and on the good, and sends rain on the righteous and on the unrighteous. For if you love those who love you, what reward do you have? Do not even the tax-collectors do the same? And if you greet only your brothers and sisters, what more are you doing than others? Do not even the Gentiles do the same? Be perfect, therefore, as your heavenly Father is perfect.'

- The love Jesus lived by and encourages is a freeing love. We may find it hard to forgive, but the beginnings of forgiveness can be to pray for those we need to forgive. We may love only those who return our love, but the beginning of real love is to expect and want nothing in return. Let us pray that our love may be like the sunshine, which shines equally on all, 'neighbour and enemy'.

The Second Week of Lent

13–19 March 2022

Something to think and pray about each day this week:

The big truth of Jesus is that he is intimately united to God the Father. So following him is not just action, but prayer that leads to action. We say someone is a great Christian – he or she helps the poor. Christianity is more – it is also prayer and the Eucharist. While we are thankful for the good lives of many people, we also can say that the full Christian life includes prayer and Mass.

It also involves community – the three were called to witness and help each other remember the Lord Jesus. Community brings the word of God alive in a real way. The community of the Church brings us to fuller faith.

Prayer leads to action for others, and action leads back to prayer. We can be so close to heavenly things that we are no earthly good! Lent brings us into this mystery of the death and resurrection of the Lord – we are part of this, and we try to make life a grace for others. We can transfigure the lives of others, or disfigure. Let's be people of the transfiguration.

Donal Neary SJ,
Gospel Reflections for Sundays of Year C: Luke

The Presence of God

The more we call on God the more we can feel God's presence. Day by day we are drawn closer to the loving heart of God.

Freedom

I am free. When I look at these words in writing, they seem to create in me a feeling of awe. Yes, a wonderful feeling of freedom. Thank you, God.

Consciousness

Help me, Lord, become more conscious of your presence. Teach me to recognise your presence in others. Fill my heart with gratitude for the times your love has been shown to me through the care of others.

The Word

The word of God comes down to us through the Scriptures. May the Holy Spirit enlighten my mind and my heart to respond to the Gospel teachings.

(Please turn to the Scripture on the following pages. Inspiration points are there, should you need them. When you are ready, return here to continue.)

Conversation

Conversation requires talking and listening.

As I talk to Jesus, may I also learn to pause and listen.

I picture the gentleness in his eyes and the love in his smile.

I can be totally honest with Jesus as I tell him my worries and cares.

I will open my heart to Jesus as I tell him my fears and doubts.

I will ask him to help me place myself fully in his care, knowing that he always desires good for me.

Conclusion

Glory be to the Father, and to the Son, and to the Holy Spirit,

As it was in the beginning, is now and ever shall be,

World without end. Amen.

Sunday 13 March
Second Sunday of Lent
Luke 9:28b–36

Now about eight days after these sayings Jesus took with him Peter and John and James, and went up on the mountain to pray. And while he was praying, the appearance of his face changed, and his clothes became dazzling white. Suddenly they saw two men, Moses and Elijah, talking to him. They appeared in glory and were speaking of his departure, which he was about to accomplish at Jerusalem. Now Peter and his companions were weighed down with sleep; but since they had stayed awake, they saw his glory and the two men who stood with him. Just as they were leaving him, Peter said to Jesus, 'Master, it is good for us to be here; let us make three dwellings, one for you, one for Moses, and one for Elijah' – not knowing what he said. While he was saying this, a cloud came and overshadowed them; and they were terrified as they entered the cloud. Then from the cloud came a voice that said, 'This is my Son, my Chosen; listen to him!' When the voice had spoken, Jesus was found alone. And they kept silent and in those days told no one any of the things they had seen.

- In our journey towards God we experience high moments, spots when we find ourselves on holy ground and God shows himself. That was the state of Saint Peter as he witnessed the Transfiguration of Jesus: 'Lord, let us build here three dwellings, for you, for Moses and for Elijah'. Peter wanted the party to go on for ever. Jesus brought him down to earth, led him down the mountain, told him to stop talking about the vision and instead be ready for Calvary.

Monday 14 March
Luke 6:36–38

Be merciful, just as your Father is merciful.

'Do not judge, and you will not be judged; do not condemn, and you will not be condemned. Forgive, and you will be forgiven; give, and it will be given to you. A good measure, pressed down, shaken together, running over, will be put into your lap; for the measure you give will be the measure you get back.'

- Jesus stresses once again the primary importance of good relationships with others. The world would be a different place if we were merciful and non-condemning. Help me to stop despising, hating, judging other people.

- Lord, my poor heart is very small, and it can also be very hard. Your heart is large and also very tender and compassionate. When I try to forgive others, my heart becomes a bit more like yours, and you swamp me with your overflowing generosity. I like that!

Tuesday 15 March
Matthew 23:1–12

Then Jesus said to the crowds and to his disciples, 'The scribes and the Pharisees sit on Moses' seat; therefore, do whatever they teach you and follow it; but do not do as they do, for they do not practise what they teach. They tie up heavy burdens, hard to bear, and lay them on the shoulders of others; but they themselves are unwilling to lift a finger to move them. They do all their deeds to be seen by others; for they make their phylacteries broad and their fringes long. They love to have the place of honour at banquets and the best seats in the synagogues, and to be greeted with respect in the market-places, and to have people call them rabbi. But you are not to be called rabbi, for you have one teacher, and you are all students. And call no one your father on earth, for you have one Father – the one in heaven. Nor are you to be called instructors, for you have one instructor, the Messiah. The greatest among you will be your servant. All who exalt themselves will be humbled, and all who humble themselves will be exalted.

- Jesus' disciples are not to make a big display of religion, nor are they to seek honourable titles like 'father' and 'teacher' and 'rabbi'. Our teacher is God, and the true disciple learns only from God. I think of what it would be like for me to assume the lowest place, to really take to heart what Jesus says about humility. I begin my prayer by asking God for the help I need, humbly and sincerely.

Wednesday 16 March
Matthew 20:17–28

While Jesus was going up to Jerusalem, he took the twelve disciples aside by themselves, and said to them on the way, 'See, we are going up to Jerusalem, and the Son of Man will be handed over to the chief priests and scribes, and they will condemn him to death; then they will hand him over to the Gentiles to be mocked and flogged and crucified; and on the third day he will be raised.'

Then the mother of the sons of Zebedee came to him with her sons, and kneeling before him, she asked a favour of him. And he said to her, 'What do you want?' She said to him, 'Declare that these two sons of mine will sit, one at your right hand and one at your left, in your kingdom.' But Jesus answered, 'You do not know what you are asking. Are you able to drink the cup that I am about to drink?' They said to him, 'We are able.' He said to them, 'You will indeed drink my cup, but to sit at my right hand and at my left, this is not mine to grant, but it is for those for whom it has been prepared by my Father.'

When the ten heard it, they were angry with the two brothers. But Jesus called them to him and said, 'You know that the rulers of the Gentiles lord it over them, and their great ones are tyrants over them. It will not be so among you; but whoever wishes to be great among you must be your servant, and whoever wishes to be first among you must be your slave; just as the Son of Man came not to be served but to serve, and to give his life a ransom for many.'

- Saint Matthew elsewhere brings up this topic of what we might call 'promotion to high office': 'The disciples came to Jesus and asked, "Who is the greatest in the kingdom of heaven?"' (Matthew 18:1). And the answer is always the same: a child. A child, ideally, is never 'pushy', elbowing others out of the way; a child, ideally, is just thankful for whatever comes. Any lording it over others, Jesus warns, is only typical of what happens among the pagans.

Thursday 17 March
Saint Patrick, Bishop and Patron of Ireland
Luke 16:19–31

'There was a rich man who was dressed in purple and fine linen and who feasted sumptuously every day. And at his gate lay a poor man named Lazarus, covered with sores, who longed to satisfy his hunger with what fell from the rich man's table; even the dogs would come and lick his sores. The poor man died and was carried away by the angels to be with Abraham. The rich man also died and was buried. In Hades, where he was being tormented, he looked up and saw Abraham far away with Lazarus by his side. He called out, "Father Abraham, have mercy on me, and send Lazarus to dip the tip of his finger in water and cool my tongue; for I am in agony in these flames." But Abraham said, "Child, remember that during your lifetime you received your good things, and Lazarus in like manner evil things; but now he is comforted here, and you are in agony. Besides all this, between you and us a great chasm has been fixed, so that those who might want to pass from here to you cannot do so, and no one can cross from there to us." He said, "Then, father, I beg you to send him to my father's house – for I have five brothers – that he may warn them, so that they will not also come into this place of torment." Abraham replied, "They have Moses and the prophets; they should listen to them." He said, "No, father Abraham; but if someone goes to them from the dead, they will repent." He said to him, "If they do not listen to Moses and the prophets, neither will they be convinced even if someone rises from the dead.'"

• Without an eye for the needy around us, our life becomes self-centred and callous. Jesus is asking his listeners to open their eyes to what is around them, and to open their ears to the simple commands of the Gospel: love your neighbour.

Friday 18 March
Matthew 21:33–43.45–46

'Listen to another parable. There was a landowner who planted a vineyard, put a fence around it, dug a wine press in it, and built a watch-tower. Then he leased it to tenants and went to another country. When the harvest time had come, he sent his slaves to the tenants to collect his produce. But the tenants seized his slaves and beat one, killed another, and stoned another. Again he sent other slaves, more than the first; and they treated them in the same way. Finally he sent his son to them, saying, "They will respect my son." But when the tenants saw the son, they said to themselves, "This is the heir; come, let us kill him and get his inheritance." So they seized him, threw him out of the vineyard, and killed him. Now when the owner of the vineyard comes, what will he do to those tenants?' They said to him, 'He will put those wretches to a miserable death, and lease the vineyard to other tenants who will give him the produce at the harvest time.'

   Jesus said to them, 'Have you never read in the scriptures:
"The stone that the builders rejected
 has become the cornerstone;
this was the Lord's doing,
 and it is amazing in our eyes"?
'Therefore I tell you, the kingdom of God will be

taken away from you and given to a people that produces the fruits of the kingdom.'

When the chief priests and the Pharisees heard his parables, they realised that he was speaking about them. They wanted to arrest him, but they feared the crowds, because they regarded him as a prophet.

- One of the saddest statements in the gospels is this innocent comment of the father: 'They will respect my son.' I am frightened to think what would happen if Jesus came into our world today. His message about the kingdom of God would put him in direct opposition to so many other kingdoms. He would become an enemy to be got rid of.

Saturday 19 March
Saint Joseph, Spouse of the Blessed Virgin Mary
Matthew 1:16.18–21.24a

… and Jacob the father of Joseph the husband of Mary, of whom Jesus was born, who is called the Messiah.

Now the birth of Jesus the Messiah took place in this way. When his mother Mary had been engaged to Joseph, but before they lived together, she was found to be with child from the Holy Spirit. Her husband Joseph, being a righteous man and unwilling to expose her to public disgrace, planned to dismiss her quietly. But just when he had resolved to do this, an angel of the Lord appeared to him in a dream and said, 'Joseph, son of David, do not be afraid to take

Mary as your wife, for the child conceived in her is from the Holy Spirit. She will bear a son, and you are to name him Jesus, for he will save his people from their sins.' When Joseph awoke from sleep, he did as the angel of the Lord commanded him; he took her as his wife.

- Matthew invites us to ponder the birth of Jesus from the perspective of Joseph, the husband of Mary. He finds himself in a moral dilemma when he learns of Mary's pregnancy, which had come about 'before they lived together'. He is a righteous man who wants to do what is best for everyone and what is in harmony with the will of God. An angel is sent to enlighten him.

- Not all the decisions we are faced with in life are clearly between right and wrong. We may have to operate in morally grey areas, or in so-called 'no-win' situations (where we will be misunderstood no matter what choice we make). We need to tap into the experience of others and pray for the wisdom of God's Holy Spirit.

The Third Week of Lent

20–26 March 2022

Something to think and pray about each day this week:

Without denying the reality of human shortcoming and sinfulness, holiness is a positive prospect. The pursuit of holiness does not rob persons of their 'energy, vitality or joy' (*GE*, 32). On the contrary, it enhances these qualities to a degree of excellence that exceeds human efforts. Holiness holds out the hope of becoming what 'the Father had in mind when he created you' (*GE*, 32). Francis declares that this is the dignity of the 'deepest self'. Like a seed lying in the ground, this self needs to be nurtured and brought to blossom through the cooperation of nature and grace. This is the holy self which is never hindered by the Holy Spirit but, on the contrary, is helped and even healed in the course of a person's life history. The search for truth, beauty and goodness in a person's life is an invitation not to be fearful but a call to deeper faith, to trust that God takes nothing that is truly human from us. Growth in holiness always augments the greater good of the world and all who live within it. We need not be afraid of holiness because we are worth it in God's eyes and what the Father wants.

Kevin O'Gorman SMA, *Journeying in Joy and Gladness*

The Presence of God

'Be still, and know that I am God!' Lord, your words lead us to the calmness and greatness of your presence.

Freedom

'In these days, God taught me as a schoolteacher teaches a pupil' (Saint Ignatius). I remind myself that there are things God has to teach me yet, and I ask for the grace to hear them and let them change me.

Consciousness

How am I really feeling? Lighthearted? Heavyhearted?
    I may be very much at peace, happy to be here.
Equally, I may be frustrated, worried or angry.
I acknowledge how I really am. It is the real me whom
    the Lord loves.

The Word

God speaks to each of us individually. I listen attentively to hear what he is saying to me. Read the text a few times, then listen.
(Please turn to the Scripture on the following pages. Inspiration points are there, should you need them. When you are ready, return here to continue.)

Conversation

Do I notice myself reacting as I pray with the word of God? Do I feel challenged, comforted, angry?

Imagining Jesus sitting or standing by me, I speak out my feelings, as one trusted friend to another.

Conclusion
I thank God for these moments we have spent together and for any insights I have been given concerning the text.

Sunday 20 March
Third Sunday of Lent
Luke 13:1–9

At that very time there were some present who told him about the Galileans whose blood Pilate had mingled with their sacrifices. He asked them, 'Do you think that because these Galileans suffered in this way they were worse sinners than all other Galileans? No, I tell you; but unless you repent, you will all perish as they did. Or those eighteen who were killed when the tower of Siloam fell on them – do you think that they were worse offenders than all the others living in Jerusalem? No, I tell you; but unless you repent, you will all perish just as they did.'

Then he told this parable: 'A man had a fig tree planted in his vineyard; and he came looking for fruit on it and found none. So he said to the gardener, "See here! For three years I have come looking for fruit on this fig tree, and still I find none. Cut it down! Why should it be wasting the soil?" He replied, "Sir, let it alone for one more year, until I dig round it and put manure on it. If it bears fruit next year, well and good; but if not, you can cut it down."'

- 'Unless you repent you will all perish as they did.' Some clear words of warning from Jesus, who alerts us to the risk of feeling too satisfied with ourselves and our ways. Is there something I feel called to change, an area in my relationships I do not feel satisfied with? I ask Jesus to let me hear his words as addressed to me.

Monday 21 March
John 4:5–42

So he came to a Samaritan city called Sychar, near the plot of ground that Jacob had given to his son Joseph. Jacob's well was there, and Jesus, tired out by his journey, was sitting by the well. It was about noon.

A Samaritan woman came to draw water, and Jesus said to her, 'Give me a drink'. (His disciples had gone to the city to buy food.) The Samaritan woman said to him, 'How is it that you, a Jew, ask a drink of me, a woman of Samaria?' (Jews do not share things in common with Samaritans.) Jesus answered her, 'If you knew the gift of God, and who it is that is saying to you, "Give me a drink", you would have asked him, and he would have given you living water.' The woman said to him, 'Sir, you have no bucket, and the well is deep. Where do you get that living water? Are you greater than our ancestor Jacob, who gave us the well, and with his sons and his flocks drank from it?' Jesus said to her, 'Everyone who drinks of this water will be thirsty again, but those who drink of the water that I will give them will never be thirsty. The water that I will give will become in them a spring of water gushing up to eternal life.' The woman said to him, 'Sir, give me this water, so that I may never be thirsty or have to keep coming here to draw water.'

Jesus said to her, 'Go, call your husband, and come back.' The woman answered him, 'I have no husband.' Jesus said to her, 'You are right in saying, "I have no husband"; for you have had five husbands, and the one you have now is not your husband. What you have said is true!' The woman said to him, 'Sir, I see that you are a prophet. Our ancestors worshipped on this mountain, but you say that the place where people must worship is in Jerusalem.' Jesus said to her, 'Woman, believe me, the hour is coming when you will worship the Father neither on this mountain nor in Jerusalem. You worship what you do not know; we worship what we know, for salvation is from the Jews. But the hour is coming, and is now here, when the true worshippers will worship the Father in spirit and truth, for the Father seeks such as these to worship him. God is spirit, and those who worship him must worship in spirit and truth.' The woman said to him, 'I know that Messiah is coming' (who is called Christ). 'When he comes, he will proclaim all things to us.' Jesus said to her, 'I am he, the one who is speaking to you.'

Just then his disciples came. They were astonished that he was speaking with a woman, but no one said, 'What do you want?' or, 'Why are you speaking with her?' Then the woman left her water-jar and went back to the city. She said to the people, 'Come and see a man who told me everything I have ever done! He cannot be the Messiah, can he?' They left the city and were on their way to him.

Meanwhile the disciples were urging him, 'Rabbi, eat something.' But he said to them, 'I have food to eat that you do not know about.' So the disciples said to one another, 'Surely no one has brought him something to eat?' Jesus said to them, 'My food is to do the will of him who sent me and to complete his work. Do you not say, "Four months more, then comes the harvest"? But I tell you, look around you, and see how the fields are ripe for harvesting. The reaper is already receiving wages and is gathering fruit for eternal life, so that sower and reaper may rejoice together. For here the saying holds true, "One sows and another reaps." I sent you to reap that for which you did not labour. Others have laboured, and you have entered into their labour.'

Many Samaritans from that city believed in him because of the woman's testimony, 'He told me everything I have ever done.' So when the Samaritans came to him, they asked him to stay with them; and he stayed there for two days. And many more believed because of his word. They said to the woman, 'It is no longer because of what you said that we believe, for we have heard for ourselves, and we know that this is truly the Saviour of the world.'

- Lord, I am going about my business like the Samarian woman, and am taken aback when you accost me at the well. You interrupt my business, my getting and spending, and the routines of my day. Let me savour this encounter, imagine you probing my desires, showing you know the waywardness of my heart. At the end, like her, I am moved with such joy at meeting you that I cannot keep it to myself. 'Lift up your eyes and see how the fields are already white for harvest.'

Tuesday 22 March
Matthew 18:21–35

Then Peter came and said to him, 'Lord, if another member of the church sins against me, how often should I forgive? As many as seven times?' Jesus said to him, 'Not seven times, but, I tell you, seventy-seven times.

'For this reason the kingdom of heaven may be compared to a king who wished to settle accounts with his slaves. When he began the reckoning, one who owed him ten thousand talents was brought to him; and, as he could not pay, his lord ordered him to be sold, together with his wife and children and all his possessions, and payment to be made. So the slave fell on his knees before him, saying, "Have patience with me, and I will pay you everything." And out of pity for him, the lord of that slave released him and forgave him the debt. But that same slave, as he went out, came upon one of his fellow-slaves who owed him a hundred denarii; and seizing him by the throat, he said, "Pay what you owe." Then his fellow-slave fell down and pleaded with him, "Have patience with me, and I will pay you." But he refused; then he went and threw him into prison until he should pay the debt. When his fellow-slaves saw what had happened, they were greatly distressed, and they went and reported to their lord all that had taken place. Then his lord summoned him and said to him, "You wicked slave! I forgave you all that debt because you pleaded with me. Should you not have had mercy on your fellow-slave, as I had mercy on you?" And in anger his lord handed him over to be tortured until he should pay his entire debt. So my heavenly Father will also do to every one of you, if you do not forgive your brother or sister from your heart.'

- This parable is about the mercy of God, which is one of the strongest divine qualities, if we may put it like that. Nothing except mercy born of compassion cancels a debt like the one referred to in the story. It further ends by calling us to be merciful as we have received mercy. Mercy is deeper than forgiveness; it sees into the heart of the other and walks around for a while in the other's shoes. It includes compassion and active healing. Shakespeare's description still resounds, '[Mercy] is twice blessed: it blesseth him that gives and him that takes.' To live in an environment of mercy is to live in an atmosphere of peace, healing and growth.

Wednesday 23 March
Matthew 5:17–19

'Do not think that I have come to abolish the law or the prophets; I have come not to abolish but to fulfil. For truly I tell you, until heaven and earth pass away, not one letter, not one stroke of a letter, will pass from the law until all is accomplished. Therefore, whoever breaks one of the least of these commandments, and teaches others to do the same, will be called least in the kingdom of heaven; but whoever does them and teaches them will be called great in the kingdom of heaven.'

- Jesus teaches by word and action, by saying and doing. His example of life is our guide and our encouragement. There is a link between what we say and what we do, and when this link is strong, we are strong in the kingdom of God. We are 'to walk it as we talk it'. Sincerity and integrity of life are what we are called to.

Thursday 24 March
Luke 11:14–23

Now he was casting out a demon that was mute; when the demon had gone out, the one who had been mute spoke, and the crowds were amazed. But some of them said, 'He casts out demons by Beelzebul, the ruler of the demons.' Others, to test him, kept demanding from him a sign from heaven. But he knew what they were thinking and said to them, 'Every kingdom divided against itself becomes a desert, and house falls on house. If Satan also is divided against himself, how will his kingdom stand? – for you say that I cast out the demons by Beelzebul. Now if I cast out the demons by Beelzebul, by whom do your exorcists cast them out? Therefore they will be your judges. But if it is by the finger of God that I cast out the demons, then the kingdom of God has come to you. When a strong man, fully armed, guards his castle, his property is safe. But when one stronger than he attacks him and overpowers him, he takes away his armour in which he trusted and divides his plunder. Whoever is not with me is against me, and whoever does not gather with me scatters.'

- Some listeners, who have just witnessed Jesus curing a dumb man, refuse to think well of him, and invent a slanderous story. It prods me: do I think ill of others more readily than I credit them with good? Lord, give me the grace to see the best in others, as I'd wish them to see the best in me.

Friday 25 March
The Annunciation of the Lord
Luke 1:26–38

In the sixth month the angel Gabriel was sent by God to a town in Galilee called Nazareth, to a virgin engaged to a man whose name was Joseph, of the house of David. The virgin's name was Mary. And he came to her and said, 'Greetings, favoured one! The Lord is with you.' But she was much perplexed by his words and pondered what sort of greeting this might be. The angel said to her, 'Do not be afraid, Mary, for you have found favour with God. And now, you will conceive in your womb and bear a son, and you will name him Jesus. He will be great, and will be called the Son of the Most High, and the Lord God will give to him the throne of his ancestor David. He will reign over the house of Jacob for ever, and of his kingdom there will be no end.' Mary said to the angel, 'How can this be, since I am a virgin?' The angel said to her, 'The Holy Spirit will come upon you, and the power of the Most High will overshadow you; therefore the child to be born will be holy; he will be called Son of God. And now, your relative Elizabeth in her old age has also conceived a son; and this is the sixth month for her who was said to be barren. For nothing will be impossible with God.' Then Mary said, 'Here am I, the servant of the Lord; let it be with me according to your word.' Then the angel departed from her.

- Scripture leaves us in no doubt about God being a long-range planner – he can determine a whole series of events to come to maturity in his own good time. In fact, he has done this for the benefit of us all – planning, even before the beginning of the world, for us to become sisters and brothers of Jesus.
- For the grand plan to come to completion, the cooperation of Mary was needed. And that is why the devotion of the faithful has long believed that Mary had to be specially privileged – namely, through being herself exempted from any touch of inherited sin.

Saturday 26 March
Luke 18:9–14

He also told this parable to some who trusted in themselves that they were righteous and regarded others with contempt: 'Two men went up to the temple to pray, one a Pharisee and the other a tax-collector. The Pharisee, standing by himself, was praying thus, "God, I thank you that I am not like other people: thieves, rogues, adulterers, or even like this tax-collector. I fast twice a week; I give a tenth of all my income." But the tax-collector, standing far off, would not even look up to heaven, but was beating his breast and saying, "God, be merciful to me, a sinner!" I tell you, this man went down to his home justified rather than the other; for all who exalt themselves will be humbled, but all who humble themselves will be exalted.'

- Both men who went up to the temple to pray were good men. The Pharisee could rightly list his qualities, but unfortunately he regarded himself as better than others. None of us can say before the Almighty that I am superior to anyone.
- The tax-collector stayed at the back. He was conscious before God that he was a sinner, but pleaded for mercy. He felt humble and unworthy before the greatness of the Almighty.
- Pope Francis continually reminds us that God never tires of forgiving us, but that we tire of asking him for forgiveness.

The Fourth Week of Lent

27 March–2 April 2022

Something to think and pray about each day this week:

The front pages of the newspapers and our online newsfeeds make the world appear as if it is falling apart. God seems to be more absent than present to the world. A person of faith may begin to wonder if God's wish for the world is mere fantasy.

There are days when I pray for God's intervention in the world. The selfish satisfaction would be immense if I could just look into the eyes of those who scoff and sneer and say 'told you so'. But God seems silent and I am not getting my way.

There are occasions, I admit, when God has broken through silence. When I visited Rwanda to hear the story of people of faith who survived the genocide, I heard lots of silence broken open. One religious sister who experienced horrendous brutality and personal suffering was inspiring. I asked the obvious question, 'How did you feel about God when all this murder and brutality was going on around you – should he have intervened to stop it?' She replied without even thinking as the answer was deep within her. 'I would not put blame for this on the shoulders of God.'

Alan Hilliard, *Dipping into Lent*

The Presence of God

To be present is to arrive as one is and open up to the other.

At this instant, as I arrive here, God is present, waiting for me.

God always arrives before me, desiring to connect with me

even more than my most intimate friend.

I take a moment and greet my loving God.

Freedom

Leave me here freely all alone. / In cell where never sunlight shone. / Should no one ever speak to me. / This golden silence makes me free!

– Part of a poem by Bl. Titus Brandsma, written while he was a prisoner at Dachau concentration camp.

Consciousness

Where am I with God? With others?

Do I have something to be grateful for? Then I give thanks.

Is there something I am sorry for? Then I ask forgiveness.

The Word

I take my time to read the word of God slowly, a few times, allowing myself to dwell on anything that strikes me.

(Please turn to the Scripture on the following pages. Inspiration points are there, should you need them. When you are ready, return here to continue.)

Conversation

How has God's word moved me? Has it left me cold?
Has it consoled me or moved me to act in a new way?
I imagine Jesus standing or sitting beside me;
I turn and share my feelings with him.

Conclusion

Glory be to the Father, and to the Son, and to the Holy
    Spirit,
As it was in the beginning, is now and ever shall be,
World without end. Amen.

Sunday 27 March
Fourth Sunday of Lent
Luke 15:1–3.11–32

Now all the tax-collectors and sinners were coming near to listen to him. And the Pharisees and the scribes were grumbling and saying, 'This fellow welcomes sinners and eats with them.'

So he told them this parable:

Then Jesus said, 'There was a man who had two sons. The younger of them said to his father, "Father, give me the share of the property that will belong to me." So he divided his property between them. A few days later the younger son gathered all he had and travelled to a distant country, and there he squandered his property in dissolute living. When he had spent everything, a severe famine took place throughout that country, and he began to be in need. So he went and hired himself out to one of the citizens of that country, who sent him to his fields to feed the pigs. He would gladly have filled himself with the pods that the pigs were eating; and no one gave him anything. But when he came to himself he said, "How many of my father's hired hands have bread enough and to spare, but here I am dying of hunger! I will get up and go to my father, and I will say to him, 'Father, I have sinned against heaven and before you; I am no longer worthy to be called your son; treat me like one of your hired hands.'" So he set off and went to his father. But while he was still far off, his father saw him and was filled with compassion; he ran and put his arms around him and kissed him. Then the son said to him, "Father, I have sinned against heaven and before you; I am no longer worthy to be called your son." But the father said to his slaves, "Quickly, bring out a robe – the best one – and put it on him; put a ring on his finger and sandals on his feet. And get the fatted calf and kill it, and let us eat and celebrate; for this son of mine was dead and is alive again; he was lost and is found!" And they began to celebrate.

'Now his elder son was in the field; and when he came and approached the house, he heard music and dancing. He called one of the slaves and asked what was going on. He replied, "Your brother has come, and your father has killed the fatted calf, because he has got him back safe and sound." Then he became angry and refused to go in. His father came out and began to plead with him. But he answered his father, "Listen! For all these years I have been working like a slave for you, and I have never disobeyed your command; yet you have never given me even a young goat so that I might celebrate with my friends. But when this son of yours came back, who has devoured your property with prostitutes, you killed the fatted calf for him!" Then the father said to him, "Son, you are always with me, and all that is mine is yours. But we had to celebrate and rejoice, because this brother of yours was dead and has come to life; he was lost and has been found.'"

- The parable of the Prodigal Son gives me a picture of the steadfast love of God. There, Lord, you show how your heavenly father would appear in human form. When he welcomes back his lost son with tears of delight, kills the fatted calf, brings out the best robe, and throws a great party, it is not to please other people, but to give expression to his own overwhelming pleasure that his child has come home. You delight in me.
- Time and again God promises me goodness. I pray that my eyes may be opened to appreciate where God is working in my life.

Monday 28 March
John 4:43–54

When the two days were over, he went from that place to Galilee (for Jesus himself had testified that a prophet has no honour in the prophet's own country). When he came to Galilee, the Galileans welcomed him, since they had seen all that he had done in Jerusalem at the festival; for they too had gone to the festival.

Then he came again to Cana in Galilee where he had changed the water into wine. Now there was a royal official whose son lay ill in Capernaum. When he heard that Jesus had come from Judea to Galilee, he went and begged him to come down and heal his son, for he was at the point of death. Then Jesus said to him, 'Unless you see signs and wonders you will not believe.' The official said to him, 'Sir, come down before my little boy dies.' Jesus said to him, 'Go; your son will live.' The man believed the word that Jesus spoke to him and started on his way. As he was going down, his slaves met him and told him that his child was alive. So he asked them the hour when he began to recover, and they said to him, 'Yesterday at one in the afternoon the fever left him.' The father realised that this was the hour when Jesus had said to him, 'Your son will live.' So he himself believed, along with his whole household. Now this was the second sign that Jesus did after coming from Judea to Galilee.

- Think of the sick people for whom you have prayed. Perhaps your prayer and that of others played its part in their recovery or had no visible result. Yet no prayer is made in vain. Prayer for another strengthens bonds, softens hearts and is heard by God.
- For whom do you want to pray now? Be sure that the Lord will answer your prayer in the way that is best.

Tuesday 29 March
John 5:1–16
After this there was a festival of the Jews, and Jesus went up to Jerusalem.

Now in Jerusalem by the Sheep Gate there is a pool, called in Hebrew Beth-zatha, which has five porticoes. In these lay many invalids – blind, lame, and paralysed. One man was there who had been ill for thirty-eight years. When Jesus saw him lying there and knew that he had been there a long time, he said to him, 'Do you want to be made well?' The sick man answered him, 'Sir, I have no one to put me into the pool when the water is stirred up; and while I am making my way, someone else steps down ahead of me.' Jesus said to him, 'Stand up, take your mat and walk.' At once the man was made well, and he took up his mat and began to walk.

Now that day was a sabbath. So the Jews said to the man who had been cured, 'It is the sabbath; it is not lawful for you to carry your mat.' But he answered them, 'The man who made me well said to me, "Take up your mat and walk."' They asked him, 'Who is the man who said to you, "Take it up and walk"?' Now the man who had been healed did not know who it was, for Jesus had disappeared in the crowd that was there. Later Jesus found him in the temple and said to him, 'See, you have been made well! Do not sin any more, so that nothing worse happens to you.' The man went away and told the Jews that it was Jesus who had made him well. Therefore the Jews started persecuting Jesus, because he was doing such things on the sabbath.

- Are there sick people in your family, among your friends? Bring them one by one, before the Lord, asking him to do what is best for them. Maybe you are worried about your own health? Tell the Lord of your anxieties and leave them with him. 'Cast all your anxiety on him, because he cares for you' (1 Peter 5:7).

Wednesday 30 March
John 5:17–30
But Jesus answered them, 'My Father is still working, and I also am working.' For this reason the Jews were seeking all the more to kill him, because he was not only breaking the sabbath, but was also calling God his own Father, thereby making himself equal to God.

Jesus said to them, 'Very truly, I tell you, the Son can do nothing on his own, but only what he sees the Father doing; for whatever the Father does, the Son does likewise. The Father loves the Son and shows him all that he himself is doing; and he will show him greater works than these, so that you will be astonished. Indeed, just as the Father raises the dead and gives them life, so also the Son gives life to whomsoever he wishes. The Father judges no one but has given all judgement to the Son, so that all may honour the Son just as they honour the Father. Anyone who does not honour the Son does not honour the Father who sent him. Very truly, I tell you, anyone who hears my word and believes him who sent me has eternal life, and does not come under judgement, but has passed from death to life.

'Very truly, I tell you, the hour is coming, and is now here, when the dead will hear the voice of the Son of God, and those who hear will live. For just as the Father has life in himself, so he has granted the Son also to have life in himself; and he has given him authority to execute judgement, because he is the Son of Man. Do not be astonished at this; for the hour is coming when all who are in their graves will hear his voice and will come out – those who have done good, to the resurrection of life, and those who have done evil, to the resurrection of condemnation.

'I can do nothing on my own. As I hear, I judge; and my judgement is just, because I seek to do not my own will but the will of him who sent me.'

- The relationship between Jesus and his heavenly Father is the topic of this enigmatic passage. Jesus traces everything in his being and in his choices to their source in the Father. 'I can do nothing on my own.' 'I seek to do not my own will but the will of him who sent me' (the Father). He and his Father are intertwined in every way, so much so that they are one (John 10:30). Honour Jesus and you will be honouring the Father.

Thursday 31 March
John 5:31–47

'If I testify about myself, my testimony is not true. There is another who testifies on my behalf, and I know that his testimony to me is true. You sent messengers to John, and he testified to the truth. Not that I accept such human testimony, but I say these things so that you may be saved. He was a burning and shining lamp, and you were willing to rejoice for a while in his light. But I have a testimony greater than John's. The works that the Father has given me to complete, the very works that I am doing, testify on my behalf that the Father has sent me. And the Father who sent me has himself testified on my behalf. You have never heard his voice or seen his form, and you do not have his word abiding in you, because you do not believe him whom he has sent.

'You search the scriptures because you think that in them you have eternal life; and it is they that testify on my behalf. Yet you refuse to come to me to have life. I do not accept glory from human beings. But I know that you do not have the love of God in you. I have come in my Father's name, and you do not accept me; if another comes in his own name, you will accept him. How can you believe when you accept glory from one another and do not seek the glory that comes from the one who alone is God? Do not think that I will accuse you before the Father; your accuser is Moses, on whom you have set your hope. If you believed Moses, you would believe me, for he wrote about me. But if you do not believe what he wrote, how will you believe what I say?'

- John the Baptist fulfilled Isaiah's prophecy, that a voice would cry in the wilderness 'Prepare the way of the Lord; make straight in the desert a highway for our God'. As we make our Lenten journey, let us reflect on what we are doing to make our own crooked ways straight.

Friday 1 April
John 7:1–2.10.25–30

After this Jesus went about in Galilee. He did not wish to go about in Judea because the Jews were looking for an opportunity to kill him. Now the Jewish festival of Booths was near.

But after his brothers had gone to the festival, then he also went, not publicly but as it were in secret.

Now some of the people of Jerusalem were saying, 'Is not this the man whom they are trying to kill? And here he is, speaking openly, but they say nothing to him! Can it be that the authorities really know that this is the Messiah? Yet we know where this man is from; but when the Messiah comes, no one will know where he is from.' Then Jesus cried out as he was teaching in the temple, 'You know me, and you know where I am from. I have not come on my own. But the one who sent me is true, and you do not know him. I know him, because I am from him, and he sent me.' Then they tried to arrest him, but no one laid hands on him, because his hour had not yet come.

- How do you pray on a text like this? (1) Enter into the way Jesus must have felt within himself in his frustration and their refusal to hear his good news. This helps us to better understand the human aspect of his life and brings us closer to him as we realise how much he is like us. (2) How do you manage when people reject you and criticise you when you mean well? It can be a great help to turn to the Lord as someone who understands you from his own experience and who supports you by his friendship.

Saturday 2 April
John 7:40–53

When they heard these words, some in the crowd said, 'This is really the prophet.' Others said, 'This is the Messiah.' But some asked, 'Surely the Messiah does not come from Galilee, does he? Has not the scripture said that the Messiah is descended from David and comes from Bethlehem, the village where David lived?' So there was a division in the crowd because of him. Some of them wanted to arrest him, but no one laid hands on him.

Then the temple police went back to the chief priests and Pharisees, who asked them, 'Why did you not arrest him?' The police answered, 'Never has anyone spoken like this!' Then the Pharisees replied, 'Surely you have not been deceived too, have you? Has any one of the authorities or of the Pharisees believed in him? But this crowd, which does not know the law – they are accursed.' Nicodemus, who had gone to Jesus before, and who was one of them, asked, 'Our law does not judge people without first giving them a hearing to find out what they are doing, does it?' They replied, 'Surely you are not also from Galilee, are you? Search and you will see that no prophet is to arise from Galilee.'

Then each of them went home.

- There is a wide range of views among the Jewish people as to who Jesus really is. Notice the constant appeal to the Old Testament. We may be more convinced by what the temple police report: 'Never has anyone spoken like this!' Jesus speaks with integrity, with wisdom, and with authority. This impresses these unsophisticated men. They are able to recognise the goodness of Jesus, which was hidden from the religious leaders.

- Pope Francis teaches that we must listen to the poor and the marginalised because they have a special insight into the reality of the world and of God.

The Fifth Week of Lent

3–9 April 2020

Something to think and pray about each day this week:

[Jesus] has been betrayed, cast aside and rejected by most of humanity. He has suffered the most awful physical and emotional torture. He can see no way forward and cries out to his Father to rescue him from the ignominy of the cross. This must be one of the most heartfelt cries of anguish or loneliness that must ever have been heard on the face of the earth; it will have gone right to the heart of God. However, Jesus acknowledges his son-ship and wishes to uphold the mission of the Father for the salvation of the world. He surrenders his own will to the will of the Father and in this he finds the courage to go on, to complete the salvation story and to win true peace for himself and all humankind.

In this he has left us an example to follow – when our wills are in union with the will of the Father, we too receive the grace to live through any loneliness and to come to a new and deeper peace at the core of our souls.

Siobhán O'Keeffe SHJM, *I Am With You Always*

The Presence of God

What is present to me is what has a hold on my
  becoming.
I reflect on the presence of God always there in love.
I pause and pray that I may let God
affect my becoming in this precise moment.

Freedom

By God's grace I was born to live in freedom. Free
to enjoy the pleasures he created for me. Dear Lord,
grant that I may live as you intended, with complete
confidence in your loving care.

Consciousness

To be conscious about something is to be aware of it.
Dear Lord, help me to remember that you gave me life.
Thank you for the gift of life.
Teach me to slow down, to be still and enjoy the
pleasures created for me. To be aware of the beauty
that surrounds me: the marvel of mountains, the
calmness of lakes, the fragility of a flower petal. I need
to remember that all these things come from you.

The Word

God speaks to each of us individually. I listen attentively
to hear what he is saying to me. Read the text a few
times, then listen.

(Please turn to the Scripture on the following pages. Inspiration points are there, should you need them. When you are ready, return here to continue.)

Conversation

I begin to talk with Jesus about the Scripture I have just read. What part of it strikes a chord in me? Perhaps the words of a friend – or some story I have heard recently – will rise to the surface in my consciousness. If so, does the story throw light on what the Scripture passage may be saying to me?

Conclusion

Glory be to the Father, and to the Son, and to the Holy
    Spirit,
As it was in the beginning, is now and ever shall be,
World without end. Amen.

Sunday 3 April
Fifth Sunday of Lent
John 8:1–11

Early in the morning he came again to the temple. All the people came to him and he sat down and began to teach them. The scribes and the Pharisees brought a woman who had been caught in adultery; and making her stand before all of them, they said to him, 'Teacher, this woman was caught in the very act of committing adultery. Now in the law Moses commanded us to stone such women. Now what do you say?' They said this to test him, so that they might have some charge to bring against him. Jesus bent down and wrote with his finger on the ground. When they kept on questioning him, he straightened up and said to them, 'Let anyone among you who is without sin be the first to throw a stone at her.' And once again he bent down and wrote on the ground. When they heard it, they went away, one by one, beginning with the elders; and Jesus was left alone with the woman standing before him. Jesus straightened up and said to her, 'Woman, where are they? Has no one condemned you?' She said, 'No one, sir.' And Jesus said, 'Neither do I condemn you. Go your way, and from now on do not sin again.'

- A meeting with Jesus is always a life-giving experience, as he himself has said, 'I am the Way, the Truth and the Life'.

Monday 4 April
John 8:12–20

Again Jesus spoke to them, saying, 'I am the light of the world. Whoever follows me will never walk in darkness but will have the light of life.' Then the Pharisees said to him, 'You are testifying on your own behalf; your testimony is not valid.' Jesus answered, 'Even if I testify on my own behalf, my testimony is valid because I know where I have come from and where I am going, but you do not know where I come from or where I am going. You judge by human standards; I judge no one. Yet even if I do judge, my judgement is valid; for it is not I alone who judge, but I and the Father who sent me. In your law it is written that the testimony of two witnesses is valid. I testify on my own behalf, and the Father who sent me testifies on my behalf.' Then they said to him, 'Where is your Father?' Jesus answered, 'You know neither me nor my Father. If you knew me, you would know my Father also.' He spoke these words while he was teaching in the treasury of the temple, but no one arrested him, because his hour had not yet come.

- No matter how dark things may seem, I remind myself that darkness can never overpower light. I turn to Christ, the light of the world.

- I pray in the words of Saint Benedict: 'O gracious and Holy Father, give us wisdom to perceive you, diligence to seek you, patience to wait for you, eyes to behold you, a heart to meditate upon you, and a life to proclaim you; through the power of the Spirit of Jesus Christ our Lord.'

Tuesday 5 April
John 8:21–30

Again he said to them, 'I am going away, and you will search for me, but you will die in your sin. Where I am going, you cannot come.' Then the Jews said, 'Is he going to kill himself? Is that what he means by saying, "Where I am going, you cannot come"?' He said to them, 'You are from below, I am from above; you are of this world, I am not of this world. I told you that you would die in your sins, for you will die in your sins unless you believe that I am he.' They said to him, 'Who are you?' Jesus said to them, 'Why do I speak to you at all? I have much to say about you and much to condemn; but the one who sent me is true, and I declare to the world what I have heard from him.' They did not understand that he was speaking to them about the Father. So Jesus said, 'When you have lifted up the Son of Man, then you will realise that I am he, and that I do nothing on my own, but I speak these things as the Father instructed me. And the one who sent me is with me; he has not left me alone, for I always do what is pleasing to him.' As he was saying these things, many believed in him.

• The Father is all truth and so is the Son, who only speaks what he has learned from the source of all.

Jesus was totally in tune with his Father, in his thinking and doing. The harmony between them is total and divine.

- Jesus is aware that only when he is lifted up on the cross will his followers realise who he is. The cross reveals God to us.

Wednesday 6 April
John 8:31–42
Then Jesus said to the Jews who had believed in him, 'If you continue in my word, you are truly my disciples; and you will know the truth, and the truth will make you free.' They answered him, 'We are descendants of Abraham and have never been slaves to anyone. What do you mean by saying, "You will be made free"?'

Jesus answered them, 'Very truly, I tell you, everyone who commits sin is a slave to sin. The slave does not have a permanent place in the household; the son has a place there for ever. So if the Son makes you free, you will be free indeed. I know that you are descendants of Abraham; yet you look for an opportunity to kill me, because there is no place in you for my word. I declare what I have seen in the Father's presence; as for you, you should do what you have heard from the Father.'

They answered him, 'Abraham is our father.' Jesus said to them, 'If you were Abraham's children, you would be doing what Abraham did, but now you are trying to kill me, a man who has told you the truth that

I heard from God. This is not what Abraham did. You are indeed doing what your father does.' They said to him, 'We are not illegitimate children; we have one father, God himself.' Jesus said to them, 'If God were your Father, you would love me, for I came from God and now I am here. I did not come on my own, but he sent me.'

- John shows the people who listened to Jesus as being prickly and precious, quick to defend their religion and righteousness. Jesus' replies show them that they have forgotten love and relationship.

Thursday 7 April
John 8:51–59
'Very truly, I tell you, whoever keeps my word will never see death.' The Jews said to him, 'Now we know that you have a demon. Abraham died, and so did the prophets; yet you say, "Whoever keeps my word will never taste death." Are you greater than our father Abraham, who died? The prophets also died. Who do you claim to be?' Jesus answered, 'If I glorify myself, my glory is nothing. It is my Father who glorifies me, he of whom you say, "He is our God", though you do not know him. But I know him; if I were to say that I do not know him, I would be a liar like you. But I do know him and I keep his word. Your ancestor Abraham rejoiced that he would see my day; he saw it and was glad.' Then the Jews said to him, 'You are not

yet fifty years old, and have you seen Abraham?' Jesus said to them, 'Very truly, I tell you, before Abraham was, I am.' So they picked up stones to throw at him, but Jesus hid himself and went out of the temple.

- Abraham's life marks the beginning of salvation history. His immense journey through the wilderness was made in response to God's call. The biblical desert was a place of passage and purification. In our own passage to the Promised Land, we must learn that God is with us at every stage of the journey, as he was with Abraham.

- Only by making ourselves vulnerable to our own pain and fear can we make ourselves open to the experience of loving and being loved.

Friday 8 April
John 10:31–42

The Jews took up stones again to stone him. Jesus replied, 'I have shown you many good works from the Father. For which of these are you going to stone me?' The Jews answered, 'It is not for a good work that we are going to stone you, but for blasphemy, because you, though only a human being, are making yourself God.' Jesus answered, 'Is it not written in your law, "I said, you are gods"? If those to whom the word of God came were called "gods" – and the scripture cannot be annulled – can you say that the one whom the Father has sanctified and sent into the world is blaspheming because I said, "I am God's Son"? If I am not doing the works of my Father, then do not believe me. But if I do them, even though you do not believe me, believe the works, so that you may know and understand that the Father is in me and I am in the Father.' Then they tried to arrest him again, but he escaped from their hands.

He went away again across the Jordan to the place where John had been baptising earlier, and he remained there. Many came to him, and they were saying, 'John performed no sign, but everything that John said about this man was true.' And many believed in him there.

- The people in today's reading condemn Jesus because of their particular image of God. What is my image of God? The best image is to see God as Pure Love. Have I ever condemned someone because I nursed a warped image of God?

Saturday 9 April
John 11:45–56

Many of the Jews therefore, who had come with Mary and had seen what Jesus did, believed in him. But some of them went to the Pharisees and told them what he had done. So the chief priests and the Pharisees called a meeting of the council, and said, 'What are we to do? This man is performing many signs. If we let him go on like this, everyone will believe in him, and the Romans will come and destroy both our holy place and our nation.' But one of them, Caiaphas, who was high priest that year, said to them, 'You know nothing at all! You do not understand that it is better for you to have one man die for the people than to have the whole nation destroyed.' He did not say this on his own, but being high priest that year he prophesied that Jesus was about to die for the nation, and not for the nation only, but to gather into one the dispersed children of God. So from that day on they planned to put him to death.

Jesus therefore no longer walked about openly among the Jews, but went from there to a town called Ephraim in the region near the wilderness; and he remained there with the disciples.

Now the Passover of the Jews was near, and many went up from the country to Jerusalem before the Passover to purify themselves. They were looking for Jesus and were asking one another as they stood in the temple, 'What do you think? Surely he will not come to the festival, will he?'

- Pope Francis, reflecting on this text, noted that Jesus died for his people and for everyone. But this, the pope stressed, must not be applied generically; it means that Jesus died specifically for each and every one of us individually. And this is the ultimate expression of Jesus' love for all people.

Holy Week

10–16 April 2022

Something to think and pray about each day this week:

Icons of Christ usually show him wearing a blue mantle over a red robe. Red signifies his humanity, the colour of the reddish earth from which Adam was made (Genesis 25:25). His humanity is in essence with his divinity, generally represented as blue, sometimes using crushed *lapis lazuli,* a most expensive mineral, at that time mined only in Afghanistan. There is little difference between the red and the blue, as though the humanity is showing through in greater clarity. As well as symbolising life, blood, passion and love in iconography in general, red has also come to symbolise the life-blood of Christ, poured out for us. The resurrection, too, is associated with red to proclaim Christ's victory of life over death. The iconographer invites us to contemplate the resurrection and the offer of eternal life to all people, extending beyond the Jewish people, although we know that God's promise to them is never rescinded and God's relationship with them remains true for all time.

Magdalen Lawler SND,
Well of Living Water: Jesus and the Samaritan Woman

The Presence of God

'Be still, and know that I am God!' Lord, your words lead us to the calmness and greatness of your presence.

Freedom

Everything has the potential to draw forth from me a fuller love and life. Yet my desires are often fixed, caught, on illusions of fulfilment. I ask that God, through my freedom, may orchestrate my desires in a vibrant loving melody rich in harmony.

Consciousness

I exist in a web of relationships: links to nature, people, God.

I trace out these links, giving thanks for the life that flows through them.

Some links are twisted or broken; I may feel regret, anger, disappointment.

I pray for the gift of acceptance and forgiveness.

The Word

I read the word of God slowly, a few times over, and I listen to what God is saying to me.

(Please turn to the Scripture on the following pages. Inspiration points are there, should you need them. When you are ready, return here to continue.)

Conversation
Jesus, you speak to me through the words of the gospels. May I respond to your call today. Teach me to recognise your hand at work in my daily living.

Conclusion
I thank God for these moments we have spent together and for any insights I have been given concerning the text.

Sunday 10 April
Palm Sunday of the Passion of the Lord
Luke 22:14–23:56

When the hour came, he took his place at the table, and the apostles with him. He said to them, 'I have eagerly desired to eat this Passover with you before I suffer; for I tell you, I will not eat it until it is fulfilled in the kingdom of God.' Then he took a cup, and after giving thanks he said, 'Take this and divide it among yourselves; for I tell you that from now on I will not drink of the fruit of the vine until the kingdom of God comes.' Then he took a loaf of bread, and when he had given thanks, he broke it and gave it to them, saying, 'This is my body, which is given for you. Do this in remembrance of me.' And he did the same with the cup after supper, saying, 'This cup that is poured out for you is the new covenant in my blood. But see, the one who betrays me is with me, and his hand is on the table. For the Son of Man is going as it has been determined, but woe to that one by whom he is betrayed!' Then they began to ask one another which one of them it could be who would do this.

A dispute also arose among them as to which one of them was to be regarded as the greatest. But he said to them, 'The kings of the Gentiles lord it over them; and those in authority over them are called benefactors. But not so with you; rather the greatest among you must become like the youngest, and the leader like one who serves. For who is greater, the one who is at the table or the one who serves? Is it not the one at the table? But I am among you as one who serves.

'You are those who have stood by me in my trials; and I confer on you, just as my Father has conferred on me, a kingdom, so that you may eat and drink at my table in my kingdom, and you will sit on thrones judging the twelve tribes of Israel.

'Simon, Simon, listen! Satan has demanded to sift all of you like wheat, but I have prayed for you that your own faith may not fail; and you, when once you have turned back, strengthen your brothers.' And he said to him, 'Lord, I am ready to go with you to prison and to death!' Jesus said, 'I tell you, Peter, the cock will not crow this day, until you have denied three times that you know me.'

He said to them, 'When I sent you out without a purse, bag, or sandals, did you lack anything?' They said, 'No, not a thing.' He said to them, 'But now, the one who has a purse must take it, and likewise a bag. And the one who has no sword must sell his cloak and buy one. For I tell you, this scripture must be fulfilled in me, "And he was counted among the lawless"; and indeed what is written about me is being fulfilled.' They said, 'Lord, look, here are two swords.' He replied, 'It is enough.'

He came out and went, as was his custom, to the Mount of Olives; and the disciples followed him. When he reached the place, he said to them, 'Pray that you may not come into the time of trial.' Then he withdrew from them about a stone's throw, knelt down, and prayed, 'Father, if you are willing, remove this cup from me; yet, not my will but yours be done.' [Then an angel from heaven appeared to him and gave him strength. In his anguish he prayed more earnestly, and his sweat became like great drops of blood falling down on the ground.] When he got up from prayer, he came to the disciples and found them sleeping because of grief, and he said to them, 'Why are you sleeping? Get up and pray that you may not come into the time of trial.'

While he was still speaking, suddenly a crowd came, and the one called Judas, one of the twelve, was leading them. He approached Jesus to kiss him; but Jesus said to him, 'Judas, is it with a kiss that you are betraying the Son of Man?' When those who were around him saw what was coming, they asked, 'Lord, should we strike with the sword?' Then one of them struck the slave of the high priest and cut off his right ear. But Jesus said, 'No more of this!' And he touched his ear and healed him. Then Jesus said to the chief priests, the officers of the temple police, and the elders who had come for him, 'Have you come out with swords and clubs as if I were a bandit? When I was with you day after day in the temple, you did not lay hands on me. But this is your hour, and the power of darkness!'

Then they seized him and led him away, bringing him into the high priest's house. But Peter was following at a distance. When they had kindled a fire in the middle of the courtyard and sat down together, Peter sat among them. Then a servant-girl, seeing him in the firelight, stared at him and said, 'This man also was with him.' But he denied it, saying, 'Woman, I do not know him.' A little later someone else, on seeing him, said, 'You also are one of them.' But Peter said, 'Man, I am not!' Then about an hour later yet another kept insisting, 'Surely this man also was with him; for he is a Galilean.' But Peter said, 'Man, I do not know what you are talking about!' At that moment, while he was still speaking, the cock crowed. The Lord turned and looked at Peter. Then Peter remembered the word of the Lord, how he had said to him, 'Before the cock crows today, you will deny me three times.' And he went out and wept bitterly.

Now the men who were holding Jesus began to mock him and beat him; they also blindfolded him and kept asking him, 'Prophesy! Who is it that struck you?' They kept heaping many other insults on him.

When day came, the assembly of the elders of the people, both chief priests and scribes, gathered together, and they brought him to their council. They said, 'If you are the Messiah, tell us.' He replied, 'If I tell you, you will not believe; and if I question you, you will not answer. But from now on the Son of Man will be seated at the right hand of the power of God.' All of them asked, 'Are you, then, the Son of God?' He said to them, 'You say that I am.' Then they said, 'What further testimony do we need? We have heard it ourselves from his own lips!'

Then the assembly rose as a body and brought Jesus before Pilate. They began to accuse him, saying, 'We found this man perverting our nation, forbidding us to pay taxes to the emperor, and saying that he himself is the Messiah, a king.' Then Pilate asked him, 'Are you the king of the Jews?' He answered, 'You say so.' Then Pilate said to the chief priests and the crowds, 'I find no basis for an accusation against this man.' But they were insistent and said, 'He stirs up the people by teaching throughout all Judea, from Galilee where he began even to this place.'

When Pilate heard this, he asked whether the man was a Galilean. And when he learned that he was under Herod's jurisdiction, he sent him off to Herod, who was himself in Jerusalem at that time. When Herod saw Jesus, he was very glad, for he had been wanting to see him for a long time, because he had heard about him and was hoping to see him perform some sign. He questioned him at some length, but Jesus gave him no answer. The chief priests and the scribes stood by, vehemently accusing him. Even Herod with his soldiers treated him with contempt and mocked him; then he put an elegant robe on him, and sent him back to Pilate. That same day Herod and Pilate became friends with each other; before this they had been enemies.

Pilate then called together the chief priests, the leaders, and the people, and said to them, 'You brought me this man as one who was perverting the people; and here I have examined him in your presence and have not found this man guilty of any of your charges against him. Neither has Herod, for he sent him back to us. Indeed, he has done nothing to deserve death. I will therefore have him flogged and release him.'

Then they all shouted out together, 'Away with this fellow! Release Barabbas for us!' (This was a man who had been put in prison for an insurrection that had taken place in the city, and for murder.) Pilate, wanting to release Jesus, addressed them again; but they kept shouting, 'Crucify, crucify him!' A third time he said to them, 'Why, what evil has he done? I have found in him no ground for the sentence of death; I will therefore have him flogged and then release him.' But they kept urgently demanding with loud shouts that he should be crucified; and their voices prevailed. So Pilate gave his verdict that their demand should be granted. He released the man they asked for, the one who had been put in prison for insurrection and murder, and he handed Jesus over as they wished.

As they led him away, they seized a man, Simon of Cyrene, who was coming from the country, and they laid the cross on him, and made him carry it behind Jesus. A great number of the people followed him, and among them were women who were beating their breasts and wailing for him. But Jesus turned to them and said, 'Daughters of Jerusalem, do not weep for me, but weep for yourselves and for your children. For the days are surely coming when they will say, "Blessed are the barren, and the wombs that never bore, and the breasts that never nursed." Then they will begin to say to the mountains, "Fall on us"; and to the hills, "Cover us." For if they do this when the wood is green, what will happen when it is dry?'

Two others also, who were criminals, were led away to be put to death with him. When they came to the place that is called The Skull, they crucified Jesus there with the criminals, one on his right and one on his left. [Then Jesus said, 'Father, forgive them; for they do not know what they are doing.'] And they cast lots to divide his clothing. And the people stood by, watching; but the leaders scoffed at him, saying, 'He saved others; let him save himself if he is the Messiah of God, his chosen one!' The soldiers also mocked him, coming up and offering him sour wine, and saying, 'If you are the King of the Jews, save yourself!' There was also an inscription over him, 'This is the King of the Jews.'

One of the criminals who were hanged there kept deriding him and saying, 'Are you not the Messiah? Save yourself and us!' But the other rebuked him, saying, 'Do you not fear God, since you are under the same sentence of condemnation? And we indeed have been condemned justly, for we are getting what we deserve for our deeds, but this man has done nothing wrong.' Then he said, 'Jesus, remember me when you come into your kingdom.' He replied, 'Truly I tell you, today you will be with me in Paradise.'

It was now about noon, and darkness came over the whole land until three in the afternoon, while the sun's light failed; and the curtain of the temple was torn in two. Then Jesus, crying with a loud voice, said, 'Father, into your hands I commend my spirit.' Having said this, he breathed his last. When the centurion saw what had taken place, he praised God and said, 'Certainly this man was innocent.' And when all the crowds who had gathered there for this spectacle saw what had taken place, they returned home, beating their breasts. But all his acquaintances, including the women who had followed him from Galilee, stood at a distance, watching these things.

Now there was a good and righteous man named Joseph, who, though a member of the council, had not agreed to their plan and action. He came from the Jewish town of Arimathea, and he was waiting expectantly for the kingdom of God. This man went to Pilate and asked for the body of Jesus. Then he took it down, wrapped it in a linen cloth, and laid it in a rock-hewn tomb where no one had ever been laid. It was the day of Preparation, and the sabbath was beginning. The women who had come with him from Galilee followed, and they saw the tomb and how his body was laid. Then they returned, and prepared spices and ointments.

On the sabbath they rested according to the commandment.

- As we go through this day and this week, let us look very carefully at Jesus our Saviour. We watch not just to admire but also to learn, to penetrate the mind, the thinking, the attitudes and the values of Jesus so that we, in the very different circumstances of our own lives, may walk in his footsteps.

Monday 11 April
Luke 4:16–21

When he came to Nazareth, where he had been brought up, he went to the synagogue on the sabbath day, as was his custom. He stood up to read, and the scroll of the prophet Isaiah was given to him. He unrolled the scroll and found the place where it was written:

'The Spirit of the Lord is upon me,
 because he has anointed me
to bring good news to the poor.
He has sent me to proclaim release to the captives
 and recovery of sight to the blind,
to let the oppressed go free,
to proclaim the year of the Lord's favour.'

And he rolled up the scroll, gave it back to the attendant, and sat down. The eyes of all in the synagogue were fixed on him. Then he began to say to them, 'Today this scripture has been fulfilled in your hearing.'

- Jesus lists his priorities: all who are restricted or confined are invited to freedom. I realise that I am included, called to new liberty and life. What does Jesus have in mind for me? Where is he calling me to freedom, to life?
- Jesus lived among people whose vision was narrow and who found it difficult to accept his inspired words – they were ready even to kill him. Yet he remained part of them, going to pray with them 'as was his custom'.

Tuesday 12 April
John 13:21–33.36–38

After saying this Jesus was troubled in spirit, and declared, 'Very truly, I tell you, one of you will betray me.' The disciples looked at one another, uncertain of whom he was speaking. One of his disciples – the one whom Jesus loved – was reclining next to him; Simon Peter therefore motioned to him to ask Jesus of whom he was speaking. So while reclining next to Jesus, he asked him, 'Lord, who is it?' Jesus answered, 'It is the one to whom I give this piece of bread when I have dipped it in the dish.' So when he had dipped the piece of bread, he gave it to Judas son of Simon Iscariot. After he received the piece of bread, Satan entered into him. Jesus said to him, 'Do quickly what you are going to do.' Now no one at the table knew why he said this to him. Some thought that, because Judas had the common purse, Jesus was telling him, 'Buy what we need for the festival'; or, that he should give something to the poor. So, after receiving the piece of bread, he immediately went out. And it was night.

When he had gone out, Jesus said, 'Now the Son of Man has been glorified, and God has been glorified in him. If God has been glorified in him, God will also glorify him in himself and will glorify him at once. Little children, I am with you only a little longer. You will look for me; and as I said to the Jews so now I say to you, "Where I am going, you cannot come."

Simon Peter said to him, 'Lord, where are you going?' Jesus answered, 'Where I am going, you cannot follow me now; but you will follow afterwards.' Peter said to him, 'Lord, why can I not follow you now? I will lay down my life for you.' Jesus answered, 'Will you lay down your life for me? Very truly, I tell you, before the cock crows, you will have denied me three times.'

- We rightly hesitate to answer affirmatively the question, 'Will you lay down your life for me?' But there is no ambivalence in Jesus – he has already decided to lay down his life for us, in purest love.

Wednesday 13 April
Matthew 26:14–25

Then one of the twelve, who was called Judas Iscariot, went to the chief priests and said, 'What will you give me if I betray him to you?' They paid him thirty pieces of silver. And from that moment he began to look for an opportunity to betray him.

On the first day of Unleavened Bread the disciples came to Jesus, saying, 'Where do you want us to make the preparations for you to eat the Passover?' He said, 'Go into the city to a certain man, and say to him, "The Teacher says, My time is near; I will keep the Passover at your house with my disciples."' So the disciples did as Jesus had directed them, and they prepared the Passover meal.

When it was evening, he took his place with the twelve; and while they were eating, he said, 'Truly I tell you, one of you will betray me.' And they became greatly distressed and began to say to him one after another, 'Surely not I, Lord?' He answered, 'The one who has dipped his hand into the bowl with me will betray me. The Son of Man goes as it is written of him, but woe to that one by whom the Son of Man is betrayed! It would have been better for that one not to have been born.' Judas, who betrayed him, said, 'Surely not I, Rabbi?' He replied, 'You have said so.'

- This highlights the depth of love that Jesus shows. He 'goes to his fate', but he is loyal all the way. He does not retaliate, no matter how shamefully he is treated. A higher love – divine love – keeps him going. I thank him for his greatness of heart, and ask that I may never betray him or his values. He promises to help me.

Thursday 14 April
Holy Thursday
John 13:1–15

Now before the festival of the Passover, Jesus knew that his hour had come to depart from this world and go to the Father. Having loved his own who were in the world, he loved them to the end. The devil had already put it into the heart of Judas son of Simon Iscariot to betray him. And during supper Jesus, knowing that the Father had given all things into his hands, and that he had come from God and was going to God, got up from the table, took off his outer robe, and tied a towel around himself. Then he poured water into a basin and began to wash the disciples' feet and to wipe them with the towel that was tied around him. He came to Simon Peter, who said to him, 'Lord, are you going to wash my feet?' Jesus answered, 'You do not know now what I am doing, but later you will understand.' Peter said to him, 'You will never wash my feet.' Jesus answered, 'Unless I wash you, you have no share with me.' Simon Peter said to him, 'Lord, not my feet only but also my hands and my head!' Jesus said to him, 'One who has bathed does not need to wash, except for the feet, but is entirely clean. And you are clean, though not all of you.' For he knew who was to betray him; for this reason he said, 'Not all of you are clean.'

After he had washed their feet, had put on his robe, and had returned to the table, he said to them, 'Do you know what I have done to you? You call me Teacher and Lord – and you are right, for that is what I am. So if I, your Lord and Teacher, have washed your feet, you also ought to wash one another's feet. For I have set you an example, that you also should do as I have done to you.

- Jesus' instruction – to do to others what he does to us – was not intended to stop at the church door. How can I bear witness to a servant God in my life today?

Friday 15 April
Good Friday
John 18:1–19:42
After Jesus had spoken these words, he went out with his disciples across the Kidron valley to a place where there was a garden, which he and his disciples entered. Now Judas, who betrayed him, also knew the place, because Jesus often met there with his disciples. So Judas brought a detachment of soldiers together with police from the chief priests and the Pharisees, and they came there with lanterns and

torches and weapons. Then Jesus, knowing all that was to happen to him, came forward and asked them, 'For whom are you looking?' They answered, 'Jesus of Nazareth.' Jesus replied, 'I am he.' Judas, who betrayed him, was standing with them. When Jesus said to them, 'I am he', they stepped back and fell to the ground. Again he asked them, 'For whom are you looking?' And they said, 'Jesus of Nazareth.' Jesus answered, 'I told you that I am he. So if you are looking for me, let these men go.' This was to fulfil the word that he had spoken, 'I did not lose a single one of those whom you gave me.' Then Simon Peter, who had a sword, drew it, struck the high priest's slave, and cut off his right ear. The slave's name was Malchus. Jesus said to Peter, 'Put your sword back into its sheath. Am I not to drink the cup that the Father has given me?'

So the soldiers, their officer, and the Jewish police arrested Jesus and bound him. First they took him to Annas, who was the father-in-law of Caiaphas, the high priest that year. Caiaphas was the one who had advised the Jews that it was better to have one person die for the people.

Simon Peter and another disciple followed Jesus. Since that disciple was known to the high priest, he went with Jesus into the courtyard of the high priest, but Peter was standing outside at the gate. So the other disciple, who was known to the high priest, went out, spoke to the woman who guarded the gate, and brought Peter in. The woman said to Peter, 'You are not also one of this man's disciples, are you?' He said, 'I am not.' Now the slaves and the police had made a charcoal fire because it was cold, and they were standing round it and warming themselves. Peter also was standing with them and warming himself.

Then the high priest questioned Jesus about his disciples and about his teaching. Jesus answered, 'I have spoken openly to the world; I have always taught in synagogues and in the temple, where all the Jews come together. I have said nothing in secret. Why do you ask me? Ask those who heard what I said to them; they know what I said.' When he had said this, one of the police standing nearby struck Jesus on the face, saying, 'Is that how you answer the high priest?' Jesus answered, 'If I have spoken wrongly, testify to the wrong. But if I have spoken rightly, why do you strike me?' Then Annas sent him bound to Caiaphas the high priest.

Now Simon Peter was standing and warming himself. They asked him, 'You are not also one of his disciples, are you?' He denied it and said, 'I am not.' One of the slaves of the high priest, a relative of the man whose ear Peter had cut off, asked, 'Did I not see you in the garden with him?' Again Peter denied it, and at that moment the cock crowed.

Then they took Jesus from Caiaphas to Pilate's headquarters. It was early in the morning. They themselves did not enter the headquarters, so as to avoid ritual defilement and to be able to eat the Passover. So Pilate went out to them and said, 'What accusation do you bring against this man?' They answered, 'If this man were not a criminal, we would not have handed him over to you.' Pilate said to them, 'Take him yourselves and judge him according to your law.' The Jews replied, 'We are not permitted to put anyone to death.' (This was to fulfil what Jesus had said when he indicated the kind of death he was to die.)

Then Pilate entered the headquarters again, summoned Jesus, and asked him, 'Are you the King of the Jews?' Jesus answered, 'Do you ask this on your own, or did others tell you about me?' Pilate replied, 'I am not a Jew, am I? Your own nation and the chief priests have handed you over to me. What have you done?' Jesus answered, 'My kingdom is not from this world. If my kingdom were from this world, my followers would be fighting to keep me from being handed over to the Jews. But as it is, my kingdom is not from here.' Pilate asked him, 'So you are a king?' Jesus answered, 'You say that I am a king. For this I was born, and for this I came into the world, to testify to the truth. Everyone who belongs to the truth listens to my voice.' Pilate asked him, 'What is truth?'

After he had said this, he went out to the Jews again and told them, 'I find no case against him. But you have a custom that I release someone for you at the

Passover. Do you want me to release for you the King of the Jews?' They shouted in reply, 'Not this man, but Barabbas!' Now Barabbas was a bandit.

Then Pilate took Jesus and had him flogged. And the soldiers wove a crown of thorns and put it on his head, and they dressed him in a purple robe. They kept coming up to him, saying, 'Hail, King of the Jews!' and striking him on the face. Pilate went out again and said to them, 'Look, I am bringing him out to you to let you know that I find no case against him.' So Jesus came out, wearing the crown of thorns and the purple robe. Pilate said to them, 'Here is the man!' When the chief priests and the police saw him, they shouted, 'Crucify him! Crucify him!' Pilate said to them, 'Take him yourselves and crucify him; I find no case against him.' The Jews answered him, 'We have a law, and according to that law he ought to die because he has claimed to be the Son of God.'

Now when Pilate heard this, he was more afraid than ever. He entered his headquarters again and asked Jesus, 'Where are you from?' But Jesus gave him no answer. Pilate therefore said to him, 'Do you refuse to speak to me? Do you not know that I have power to release you, and power to crucify you?' Jesus answered him, 'You would have no power over me unless it had been given you from above; therefore the one who handed me over to you is guilty of a greater sin.' From then on Pilate tried to release him, but the Jews cried out, 'If you release this man, you are no friend of the emperor. Everyone who claims to be a king sets himself against the emperor.'

When Pilate heard these words, he brought Jesus outside and sat on the judge's bench at a place called The Stone Pavement, or in Hebrew Gabbatha. Now it was the day of Preparation for the Passover; and it was about noon. He said to the Jews, 'Here is your King!' They cried out, 'Away with him! Away with him! Crucify him!' Pilate asked them, 'Shall I crucify your King?' The chief priests answered, 'We have no king but the emperor.' Then he handed him over to them to be crucified.

So they took Jesus; and carrying the cross by himself, he went out to what is called The Place of the Skull, which in Hebrew is called Golgotha. There they crucified him, and with him two others, one on either side, with Jesus between them. Pilate also had an inscription written and put on the cross. It read, 'Jesus of Nazareth, the King of the Jews.' Many of the Jews read this inscription, because the place where Jesus was crucified was near the city; and it was written in Hebrew, in Latin, and in Greek. Then the chief priests of the Jews said to Pilate, 'Do not write, "The King of the Jews", but, "This man said, I am King of the Jews."' Pilate answered, 'What I have written I have written.' When the soldiers had crucified Jesus, they took his clothes and divided them into four parts, one for each soldier. They also took his tunic; now the tunic was seamless, woven in one piece from the top. So they said to one another, 'Let us not tear it, but cast lots for it to see who will get it.' This was to fulfil what the scripture says,

'They divided my clothes among themselves,
 and for my clothing they cast lots.'

And that is what the soldiers did.

Meanwhile, standing near the cross of Jesus were his mother, and his mother's sister, Mary the wife of Clopas, and Mary Magdalene. When Jesus saw his mother and the disciple whom he loved standing beside her, he said to his mother, 'Woman, here is your son.' Then he said to the disciple, 'Here is your mother.' And from that hour the disciple took her into his own home.

After this, when Jesus knew that all was now finished, he said (in order to fulfil the scripture), 'I am thirsty.' A jar full of sour wine was standing there. So they put a sponge full of the wine on a branch of hyssop and held it to his mouth. When Jesus had received the wine, he said, 'It is finished.' Then he bowed his head and gave up his spirit.

Since it was the day of Preparation, the Jews did not want the bodies left on the cross during the sabbath, especially because that sabbath was a day of great solemnity. So they asked Pilate to have the legs of the crucified men broken and the bodies removed. Then the soldiers came and broke the legs of the first and of the other who had been crucified with him. But when they came to Jesus and saw that he was already dead, they did not break his legs. Instead, one of the soldiers pierced his side with a spear, and at once blood and water came out. (He who saw this has testified so that you also may believe. His testimony is true, and he knows that he tells the truth.) These things occurred so that the scripture might be fulfilled, 'None of his bones shall be broken.' And again another passage of scripture says, 'They will look on the one whom they have pierced.'

After these things, Joseph of Arimathea, who was a disciple of Jesus, though a secret one because of his fear of the Jews, asked Pilate to let him take away the body of Jesus. Pilate gave him permission; so he came and removed his body. Nicodemus, who had at first come to Jesus by night, also came, bringing a mixture of myrrh and aloes, weighing about a hundred pounds. They took the body of Jesus and wrapped it with the spices in linen cloths, according to the burial custom of the Jews. Now there was a garden in the place where he was crucified, and in the garden there was a new tomb in which no one had ever been laid. And so, because it was the Jewish day of Preparation, and the tomb was nearby, they laid Jesus there.

- Good Friday puts the cross before me and challenges me not to look away. If I have followed

Jesus' footsteps to Calvary, I do not have to fear because I, like him, am confident in God's enduring presence. Wherever there is suffering or pain, I look again, seeking the face of Jesus. I ask him for the strength I need to be a sign of hope wherever there is despair, to be a presence of love wherever it is most needed.

Saturday 16 April
Holy Saturday
Luke 24:1–12
But on the first day of the week, at early dawn, they came to the tomb, taking the spices that they had prepared. They found the stone rolled away from the tomb, but when they went in, they did not find the body. While they were perplexed about this, suddenly two men in dazzling clothes stood beside them. The women were terrified and bowed their faces to the ground, but the men said to them, 'Why do you look for the living among the dead? He is not here, but has risen. Remember how he told you, while he was still in Galilee, that the Son of Man must be handed over to sinners, and be crucified, and on the third day rise again.' Then they remembered his words, and returning from the tomb, they told all this to the eleven and to all the rest. Now it was Mary Magdalene, Joanna, Mary the mother of James, and the other women with them who told this to the apostles. But these words

seemed to them an idle tale, and they did not believe them. But Peter got up and ran to the tomb; stooping and looking in, he saw the linen cloths by themselves; then he went home, amazed at what had happened.

- We must not skip lightly over Holy Saturday. It is a time of waiting. I wait with Mary: we chat and pray as Jesus descends into the world of the dead. He holds the keys to Death and the Underworld. Theologians suggest that this means that Jesus went in search of the dead, especially hardened sinners. These in their despair find his footprints on their lonely path, and come face to face with the crucified One, who invites them to accept the forgiving love of God. He goes to the dark limits of human experience and brings them Easter light.